Fun i Germany

Sacha de Frisching

Illustrations by Sylvie Rainaud

English edition prepared by Claudia Eilers

© Hachette Guides Bleus 1986
Originally published under the title
L'Allemagne en salopette by Hachette, Paris.

Photoset by Parker Typesetting Service, Leicester
Printed and bound in France by
Offset Aubin, Poitiers
ISBN 0 330 29236 6

This book is sold subject to the condition that it shall not, by way of trade or otherwise be lent, re-sold, hired out or otherwise circulated without the publisher's prior consent in any form of binding or cover other than that in which it is published and without a similar condition including this condition being imposed on the subsequent purchaser

Whilst the advice and information in this book are believed to be true and accurate at the time of going to press, neither the author nor the publisher can accept any legal responsibility or liability for any errors or omissions that may be made

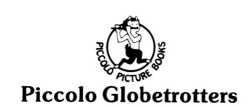

Piccolo Globetrotters

Willkommen in Deutschland

Germany is divided into two states: the Federal Republic of Germany in the west, and the German Democratic Republic in the east. Berlin, the old capital, is cut in half: West Berlin and East Berlin.

Germany lies in the heart of Europe. The three biggest rivers in West Germany are the Elbe, the Rhine and the Danube.

Come and play!
The letters of four big German
cities have been jumbled up
on the sign boards below.
Quickly put them into order!

All around the circle
you'll find the names of Germany's
neighbours – but watch out
each country is in its own language!
If you find them all in 1 minute
you're a genius!

River of legends

The Rhine is Europe's longest river.
It is so busy with boats and barges
that it's like a water-motorway.
But it is also full of mystery
with medieval castles, called **Burgen**,
towering high above the steep cliffs,
and a legendary golden-haired mermaid
whose enchanting songs
lured many a mariner
onto the treacherous rocks.

If you arrange the castles in order from the biggest to the smallest, the letters will tell you the mermaid's name. Now do the same for the boats – but this time from the smallest to the biggest and you'll discover the German word for 'ship'.

Solution: Lorelei/Schiff

Lots of capitals

A

B

In the olden days, Germany consisted of lots of independent kingdoms and duchies. Nowadays, the Federal Republic is made up of ten **Länder** (States) – or eleven if you count West-Berlin. They all have their own regional capitals which play an important role in the life of the whole nation. Here are four of them for you to discover.

We'll start with Bonn, the federal capital and seat of the government. The head of state, the Chancellor, lives here.

A forest of flags – but which belongs to the Federal Republic? You'll find the answer somewhere in this book . . .

Munich is the capital of Bavaria, a land of lakes and mountains with lots of colourful traditions. In September, they have great celebrations for the beer festival called **Oktoberfest**.

Which of these beer mugs are identical?

Solution: B and E

6

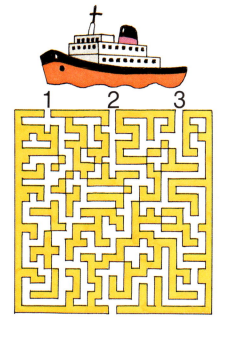

Hamburg is an international port on the river Elbe by the North Sea. Here you can see big container ships and cruise liners from all over the world.

Be a tugboat and take the ship to the right dock.

Frankfurt is one of the oldest and biggest cities. It has a huge airport, lots of 'skyscrapers' and is the banking capital.

Spot the odd coin out!

Solution: the 1976 Irish coin.

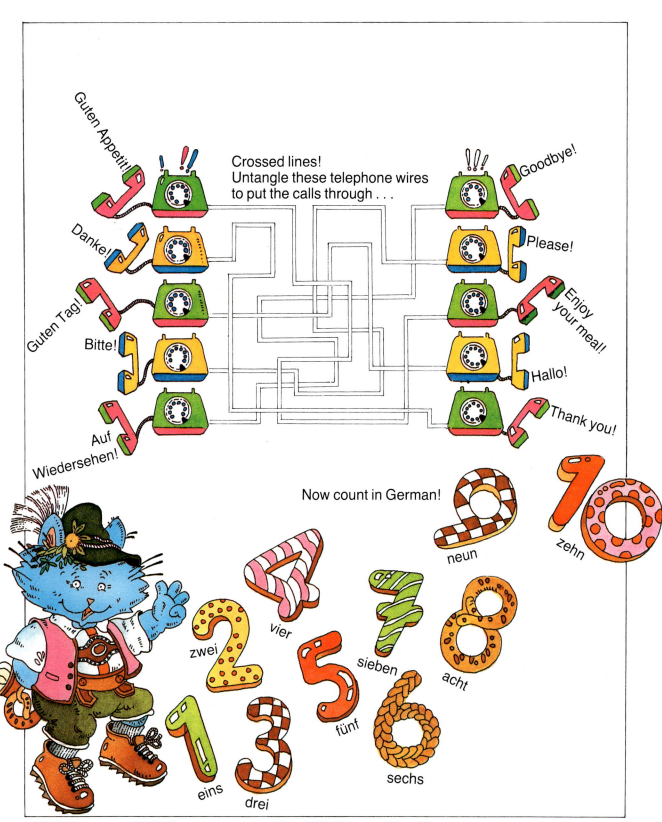

D for Deutschland

Here is an A to Z of German objects.
Starting from A, visit all of them
as quickly as possible
without taking the same path twice.

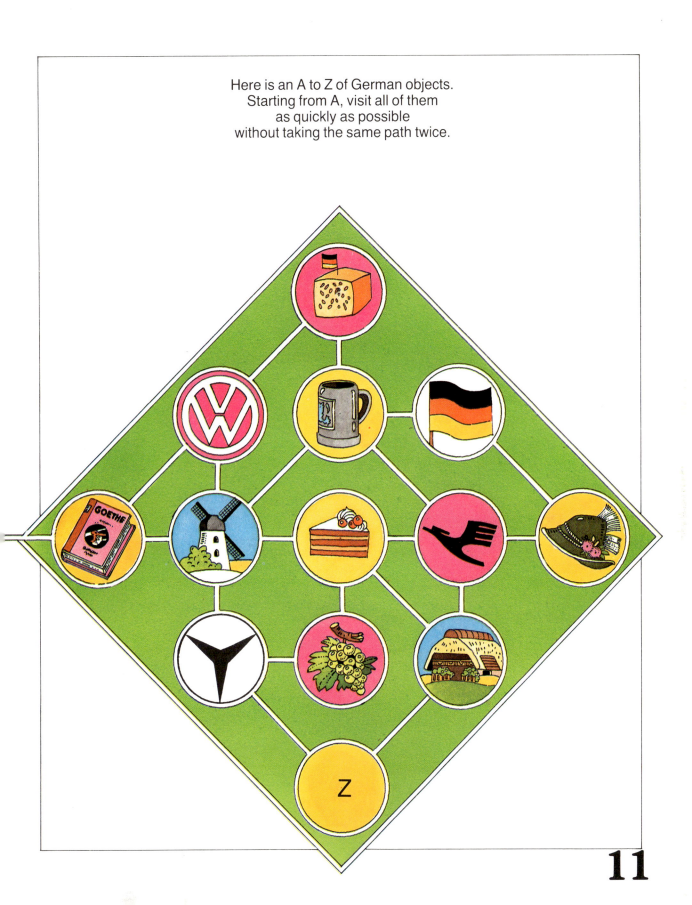

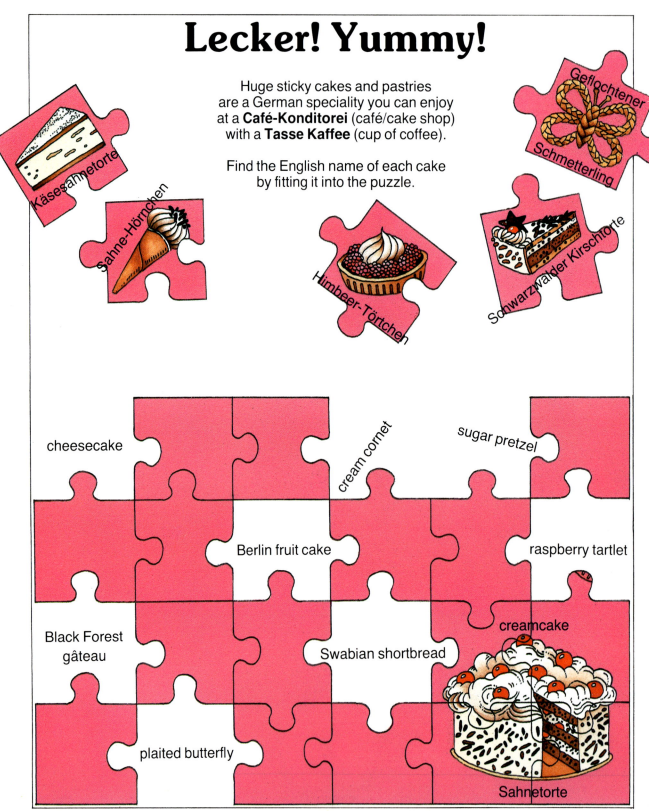

Berliner Napfkuchen

Zuckerbrezel

Schwäbische Springerle

For breakfast (**Frühstück**) or supper (**Abendessen**) Germans often eat sandwiches with cheese or cold meats. Work out what I put into mine and have fun inventing your own special sandwich made with all your favourite ingredients.

Prost! Cheers!

Beer is made from barley, hops and water. Sprouting barley grains are turned into malt which is the basis of beer.

Hops give beer its bitter flavour: only a few grammes per litre are needed. Hops are climbing plants which you can sometimes find growing wild by streams.

Here you get a good view of the inside of a brewery. Follow all the stages of beer brewing, then write the German word for beer onto this label. You'll find it in the picture!

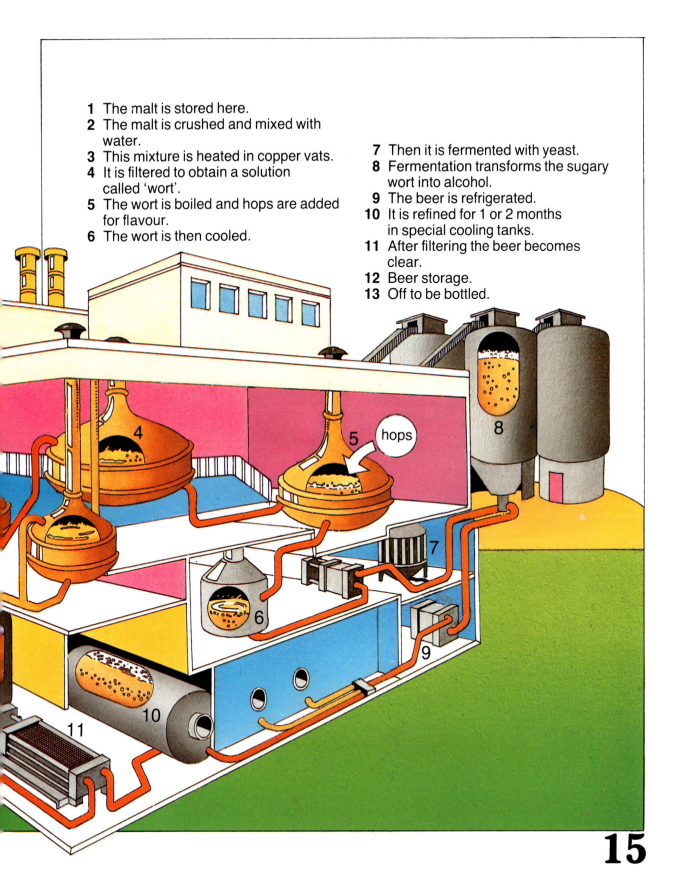

Weihnachten

The Christmas tree is a tradition which came from Germany. And there is also a song about it. This is the original version.

O Tannenbaum, o Tannenbaum,
wie treu sind deine Blätter!
Du grünst nicht nur zur Sommerzeit,
nein, auch im Winter, wenn es schneit.
O Tannenbaum, o Tannenbaum,
wie treu sind deine Blätter!

Christmas (**Weihnachten**) is a wonderful celebration in Germany. There are Christmas markets in every town square, where you can buy decorations, gingerbread, and presents for your friends.

Christmas trees are decorated with real candles, biscuits and sweets. And every child finds a bowl full of goodies under the tree on Christmas Eve.

To make your own Christmas biscuits you'll need:

1 small packet of frozen shortcrust pastry
1 egg
60 g icing sugar
sugar beads
a little flour
1 rolling pin
1 whisk
1 bowl
ribbons

1 Sprinkle some flour on to a board and roll out the pastry.

2 Cut out little angels like ours . . . and don't forget to make a hole!

3 Bake in the oven for 30 minutes.

4 Beat the eggwhite until stiff and add the sugar.

5 When the biscuits have cooled down decorate with egg-white and sugar beads.

6 Leave to dry, then tie on the ribbon for hanging on the tree.

Just my type!

In the 15th century, a German goldsmith called Gutenberg invented the printing process: he used individual letter blocks which could be fitted together to make words and then printed onto paper.

In those days, people wrote in gothic letters. This beautiful writing can still be found in Germany today on inn signs and in some books.

Write your name in gothic letters:

If you unroll the spiral, you'll discover Gutenberg's first name, the town he worked in and the title of his first book.

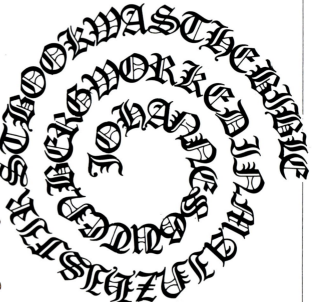

By air and rail

Do you know what was invented by Ferdinand von Zeppelin and by Werner von Siemens? You'll find out by joining the dots starting from 2 and counting in twos.

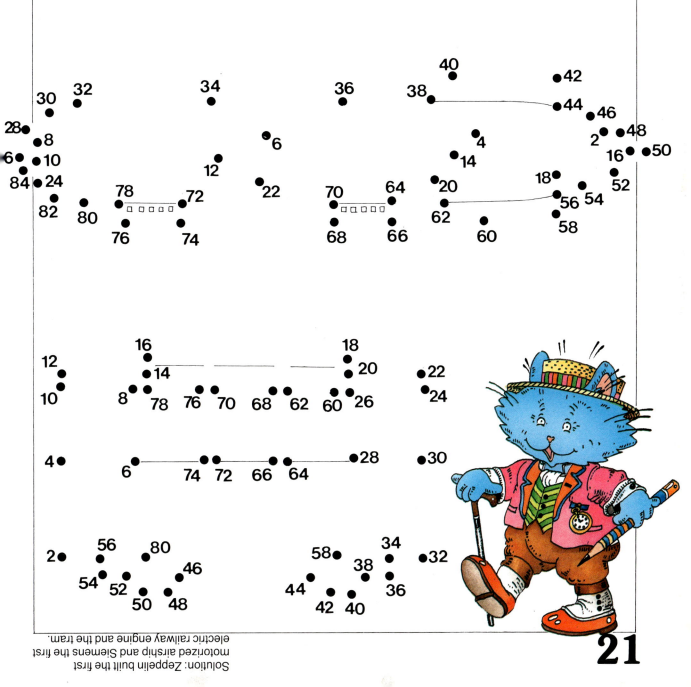

Solution: Zeppelin built the first motorized airship and Siemens the first electric railway engine and the tram.

Great minds

Here are some famous names from German history. Can you work out what each of them is known for? Draw a line between each person and the right description – and spot the odd one out!

mathematical genius

religious reformer

great emperor of Europe

Santa Claus, friend of the children

Albrecht Dürer   Albert Einstein   Mozart   Goethe

Solution: Sankt Nikolaus is the odd one out. He is a mythical person who tiptoes in during the night of December 6th, leaving sweets outside children's bedroom doors.

Musik, Musik . . .

Music plays an important part in German everyday life and many schools have their own orchestra. In the symphony orchestra every instrument has its own place. Look at these musicians and decide which instrument each of them is supposed to be playing.

Germany has many famous composers.
I'll introduce you to three of them.
Their names are hidden in this crossword.

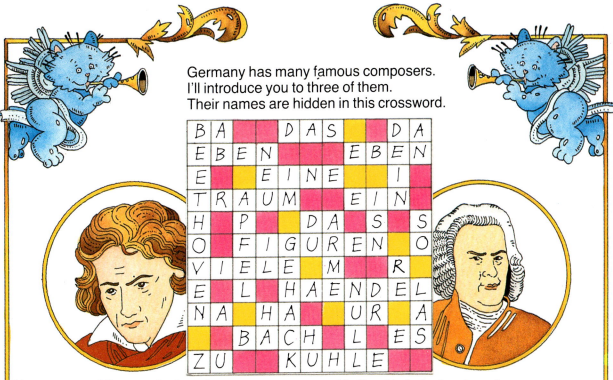

He was one of the greatest geniuses
in the history of music.
He had to abandon his career as
a pianist when he lost his hearing,
but he went on composing even though deaf!
In all he wrote 9 symphonies, 16 quartets,
32 piano sonatas and one opera.

He lived in Leipzig where he was
director of music at the two main churches.
He was a brilliant organist
and composed numerous masses,
cantatas and organ pieces.
Three of his sons became
great musicians in their turn.

He started his career in Italy
where he wrote many operas,
until he became court musician
for the King of England
for whom he composed his Water Music.
His favourite instrument was the harpsichord.

Solution: Left: Ludwig van Beethoven (1770–1827).
Right: Johann Sebastian Bach (1685–1750).
Centre: Georg Friedrich Händel (1685–1759).

25

Curtain up

Every year, opera fans from all over the world gather in Bayreuth for the Wagner Festival. Richard Wagner was a poet and a composer, and his operas were inspired by old Germanic and Nordic myths.

The legend of the Nibelungen tells of the struggle between dwarfs, gods and giants for the magic ring made from the gold of the Rhine, a metal which makes its owner invincible.
The story of Siegfried is the third episode of this legend made into four operas by Wagner.

After the death of his parents, Siegfried is brought up by the dwarf Mime, in the hope that the boy may one day win the ring for him. They live in the forest not far from the cave where the giant Fafner, now transformed into a dragon, guards the magic ring.

Siegfried, who does not know the meaning of fear, forges a powerful sword for his fight with the dragon. After a fierce struggle, he manages to kill the guardian of the ring.

As he puts his blood stained finger to his mouth, suddenly he can understand the language of the birds and is warned of Mime's evil plot to murder him in order to have the ring to himself. Siegfried kills the treacherous dwarf and takes the ring.

A bird then leads him to a rock where Brünnhilde sleeps surrounded by a circle of fire which can only be broken by a fearless hero.

Siegfried walks through the fire and awakes Brünnhilde with a kiss, thus breaking the spell put on her by the god Wotan, and puts the ring on her finger.

Top speed

All these cars are made in Germany.
How many do you recognize?
And can you draw 2 straight lines to
divide this picture into 4 parts
without touching any car?

Solution: A=BMW, B=Mercedes, C=Opel, D=Audi, E=Volkswagen, F=Porsche

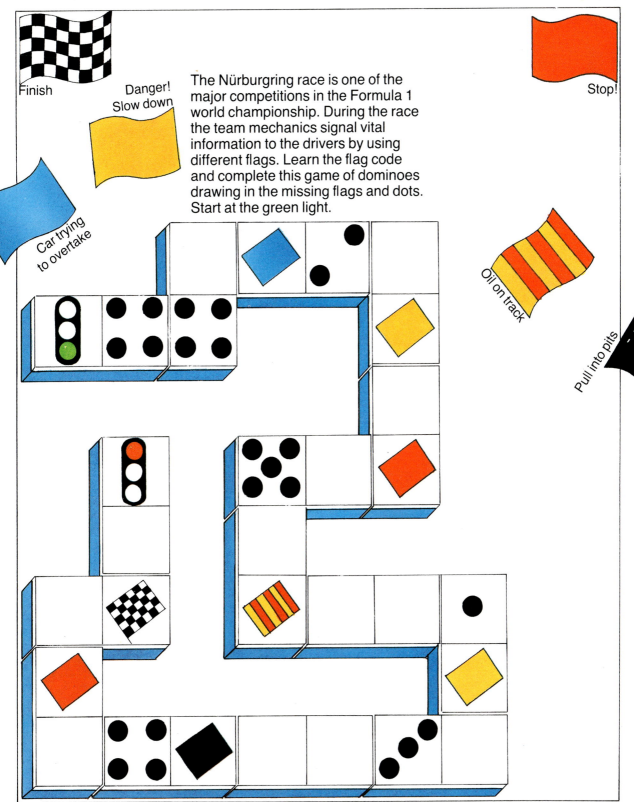

Es war einmal...
Once upon a time...

You may have heard some of Grimm's Fairy Tales – but do you know the story of the Grimms? They were two brothers called Jakob and Wilhelm who lived in Germany in the first half of the 19th century. They were very fond of each other and worked together for their entire life. They were fascinated by poetry and old legends and travelled throughout Germany to collect all the tales that were traditionally told round the hearths of village cottages. Their first book of tales, rewritten by Wilhelm was a great success in Germany and abroad. In Germany it was the most reprinted book after Luther's bible.

Jakob and Wilhelm Grimm were also great scholars, researching the origin and development of the German language and they were both made professors at Berlin University. But now look at all the characters from Grimm's tales. You are bound to recognize some of them!
Which tale does each of them belong to?

The Frog Prince
Hänsel and Gretel
Rumpelstiltskin
The Bremen Town Musicians
The Valiant Tailor
Snowwhite and the Seven Dwarfs
The Little Elves
The Drummer

Made in Germany

How about making a Bavarian souvenir to surprise a friend or amuse yourself? Cut off the pieces, join them with letter clips – and your little friend in **Lederhosen** (leather pants) will move!